Gnosis beyond "Gnosticism"

Jeremy Puma

ISBN: **1456539418**
ISBN-13: **978-1456539412**

DEDICATION

To you.

CONTENTS

ACKNOWLEDGMENTS

Thanks

0 APOLOGIA:
AGAINST A FALSE CATEGORY

I have been incredibly wrong, and the time has come to confess my errors. I have been guilty of perpetuating a falsehood: that there is an unbroken "Gnostic" tradition of some kind, and that modern "Gnosticism" is based on an ancient religion. I have been inadvertently lying to myself and to others that this is the case. Factually and historically, however, what is currently practiced as "Gnosticism" is a product of Nineteenth Century Occultism and the New Age Movement, and I can no longer in good conscience associate myself with the religion as it stands, nor can I encourage people who are interested in the spirituality of the Nag Hammadi Library[1] to become involved with organizations making the claim to the word.

---

[1] A cache of mystical Christian codices discovered in Egypt in 1945, chiefly containing writings from sects now referred to as Valentinians and Sethians.

Until quite recently, I used to think this way, and became involved in modern Gnostic circles. It was only when I started looking into the history of these organizations, and truly investigating what academics have been uncovering in the world of "Gnostic" studies, that I began to question the veracity of "Gnosticism" in its modern form.

The term "Gnosticism" was coined in the Seventeenth Century, picked up by scholars in the centuries following who had access to perhaps 20% of the material now best represented by the Nag Hammadi collection of codices ("Nag Hammadi Library, NHL"). It was then co-opted by Theosophists and other Orientalist Occultists[2], used to describe "real" Christianity as opposed to "Christianity as practiced by those other jerks." With few exceptions, the concept of "gnosis" was held to be synonymous with that of "enlightenment" of the Buddhist sort–- epiphany, if you will. This is unsurprising, given the popularity of the relatively new Eastern philosophies which had only recently been introduced in the West during the heyday of these organizations.

As it turned out, the discovery, and subsequent publication of the NHL and its scholarly analysis in academic circles has almost entirely overturned the

---

[2] See, for instance, the works of H.P. Blavatsky or 19th Century French "Gnostic" Jules Doinel.

Nineteenth Century ideas on the subject. These very analyses, however, are fairly consistently ignored within modern Gnostic circles, because they invalidate much of the Occultist/New Age nature of modern Gnostic groups. The sects represented in the Nag Hammadi Library very likely didn't even refer to themselves as Gnostic. The term "Gnostic" was used as a self-designation more frequently by "mainstream" Christians in the ancient world than by the sects represented in that collection.

At the time of this writing, there is no modern organization which designates itself "Gnostic" that is truly representative of the ideas and practices described in the Nag Hammadi Library. Gnosticism, as it exists currently, is a definitively modern invention, based more on Nineteenth Century Occultism and the New Age movement than on anything written prior to the modern era.

This statement is not a value judgment, it is a simple statement of fact. Others have proven that this is the case far more thoroughly and effectively than I could, so I refer the reader to the sources in the footnote below for the details of this argument.[3]

There are some very good people involved in

---

[3] Ismo Dunderburg, *Beyond Gnosticism: Myth, Lifestyle, and Society in the School of Valentinus;* Jesse Christopher Folks, "The New Paradigm," http://goo.gl/2ZHaG and "Gnuance I and II," goo.gl/Oegmu; Michael Williams, *Rethinking Gnosticism*

modern Gnosticism,[4] but there are just as many charlatans and egomaniacs who would rather have a seat on Oprah's couch than really understand the Nag Hammadi Library. There are spiritual guides with much to offer those interested in modern Gnosticism. There are also "priests" who are essentially role-players, who are more concerned with self-promotion and ego-gratification than honest reflection.

I would advise those involved in Modern Gnostic organizations to look at them critically, skeptically, with an eye towards history and towards power relationships. I even have it on good authority that at least one well-known Gnostic guru who is very heavily published has been guilty of pressuring members of his organizations into sexual relationships.

So, in summary, I have completely embraced the theories of Michael Williams and Karen King, who have fairly categorically imploded the idea that "Gnosticism" ever existed before the 19th Century. I refer those interested in their arguments to their works. There are those who will of course disagree– the argument has been put forth that if Gnosticism doesn't work as a category, then neither should Christianity or Buddhism. This argument is, however, misapplied– what I am suggesting is rather as though some Lutherans are claiming that Lutheranism existed in 750 AD, and claims to the

---

[4] Fr. Sam Osborne of the Ecclesia Gnostica, for example.

contrary are intended to discredit the existence of the Lutheran Church. I do very sincerely believe that there is a Gnosticism. However, I believe that Gnosticism has existed since at least the Nineteenth Century, and is the product of its age. **For this reason, in this text, when the words "Gnosticism" and "Gnostic" appear, they strictly and specifically refer to modern organizations and philosophies.**

What's it like to be confronted with the absolute certainty that one's identity for the past fifteen years has been predicated on a misunderstanding? It's a pretty huge blow, but it's also very liberating. Now I've accepted that the individuals who wrote the ancient works were not Gnostics, but instead were Christians, Sethians, Valentinians, explorers of the spirituality of information still perhaps best represented in the works of (non-Gnostic) author Philip K. Dick. I can finally embrace my skepticism towards the occultist, New Age, "neopagan" and "Goddess-centered" ideas creeping into modern Gnosticism, which are indubitably not something with which I personally wish to associate. I can reestablish in myself the Christ-centeredness that modern Gnostics seem so interested in demolishing, while at the same time continuing to pursue my interest in Buddhist theory and practice without worrying about how to integrate it into a bad category.

I have come to the conclusion that it is time to

cede the term Gnosticism to the modern organizations that want it. In spite of my previous published work, I no longer consider myself a "Gnostic."

I also want to stress that within extant Gnostic organizations, there are some excellent individuals doing some excellent work– I simply no longer consider myself a coreligionist. To paraphrase a dear friend, the belief that modern Gnosticism accurately represents some kind of classical "Gnosticism," and that it is the continuation of some kind of ancient "tradition," is a confessional, faith-based dogma that cannot be supported with fact but is purely a matter of self-identity, "like Mormons saying the natives had elephants."

In my pursuit of Gnosticism-as-a-false-category, I've been a real jerk on more than one occasion. The whole time I spent attacking modern Gnosticism as "bullshit," declaring the work of John Lash, Samael Weor and various proponents of hallucinogens "not Gnostic," I was dead wrong. I've now come to agree that these paths and organizations are indeed Gnostic, just as Gnostic as any modern organization referring to itself as such can claim to be. So, my apologies.

I also want to apologize to any members of mainstream religions I have offended with my incomplete understanding of these ancient heretical texts. I've said some pretty incredible things in the past, and pulled some whoppers right out of who knows where. I've ignored good advice from friends simply because those darned "facts" didn't fit into my Gnostic worldview. For this, I also apologize.

If you're still reading this, I beg your indulgence for my meanderings. The decisions I've explored in this Apologia have been on my mind for some time, and having finally come to fruition, needed a place to flower. I have even gone as far as to have taken most of my books off of the market, excepting the ones I think are not representative of modern Gnosticism.

This is a personal decision, and certainly not one I think needs to be taken up by everyone. For me, however, I've had enough of trying to bend historical fact and textual evidence to try to defend modernist occultism. Enough with the Movementarians– let's take solace in what we already have, and try to do so honestly and without guile.

The fact of the matter is, it is impossible to attempt any one-to-one revival of Nag Hammadi-style spiritual practice in a modern context. The ideas found therein are far too ambiguous and unclear, and the lacunae too numerous, to provide any kind of cogent understanding of the original works in their original context to any but the most learned scholar. This current work is my attempt to abandon modern "Gnosticism" in favor of a different kind of spiritual approach, one which I feel remains true to the spirit of the Nag Hammadi documents and their correlatives (the Egyptian *Hermetica*, for instance, or the contents of the *Codex Brucianus* and the *Pistis Sophia*. I hope you find it interesting.

1 INTRODUCTION

My attempt to form a spiritual approach follows
in this little work, an approach to which I simply refer
as "This Way." This Way is a Way that works. It is a
consciously designed syncretism between Christianity
and Buddhism, a context with elements of both. The
Christian elements are highly influenced by Sethian
and Valentinian Nag Hammadi streams, and the
Buddhist elements by the Zen tradition. Terms from
both streams will be used. This Way doesn't have
any kind of name; it's just a Way that happens to be
effective. You can choose to do it, or not to do it.

This Way is designed for developing gnosis
within its specific context. It is not "Gnosticism." It
was not "divinely inspired," "channeled," or any other
such stuff. It is not dependent upon any kind of
dubious "Apostolic Succession" or lineage.

It does, however, produce results.

This Way is predicated on the following formula:

Gnosis = Awakening (Word + Wisdom)

Or, G = AL + AS

Gnosis must be a deeply personal experience, but not every deeply personal experience is gnosis.

According to this contemporary approach, true gnosis (G) requires three variables:

A: An Awakening Event – This might be an epiphany, a theophany, a revelation, etc., but it must be personal and must be experienced. Way persons may participate in and perform the Christian Sacrament of the Eucharist, and perform and recognize the validity of the other Christian Sacraments. The primary practice for the cultivation of awakening, however, is contemplative. A number of contemplative practices are available to the Way person, including, but not limited to zazen, vipassana, ascent prayer, etc. A basic practice that has worked can be found on this site.

L: The Word, or Logos – An informational context into which one can place the awakening event. Remember that one of the meanings of Logos is "word," but it also means "faculty of reason," "discourse," "law," "pronouncement." Jesus Christ, as the Logos, represents the deliverer of discourse– in Buddhist terms, we may find similarities to the Buddha as the Living Dharma. In the Sethian myth,

Jesus carries forth the Discourse as an extended faculty of reason initiated in the Pleroma by the Divine Seth. The preexistent Logos within the Pleroma is the Christos, which manifests within the World of Forms as living information. He is the instructor who institutes the sacraments– information. He teaches the Way to his disciples– information. He facilitates the presence of the Nous within each of us– information.

Way persons may choose to participate in Buddhist Sanghas or Christian Congregations. They also may establish zendos in their areas, or practice as individuals.

S: Wisdom, or Sophia – The wisdom to apply the awakening event through praxis within one's holistic life. This is Sophia, tempered by faith, who carries us forward in our day-to-day existence. She delivers the essential Wisdom necessary to apply the teachings of the Logos to day-to-day life. With her infinite compassion, she descends through the spheres of the Archons to engage the spirit in each of us and allow us to develop compassion for all beings. She allows us to perform the sacraments presented by the Logos wisely, and fills our actions with content, keeping us moving forward and upward as we climb the ladder of emanations towards the realms of the Pleroma.

Wisdom manifests for the Way person via the Four Virtues– Inquiry, Compassion, Humility and

Service, and the Precepts, ethical guidelines suggested for each of us.

Ultimately, This Way produces a state best described as *ataraxia*, or *tranquility*. As you will see, this doesn't necessarily mean peacefulness, happiness, joy or bliss; however, it is the best we can reasonably accomplish while resident in this imperfect World of Forms.

PART ONE: THEORY

2 FOUNDATIONS

The following texts very substantially influenced the formation of This Way, and cannot be recommended highly enough to the reader.

The Secret Book of John, a Sethian Christian text found in the Nag Hammadi Collection

The *Shobogenzo* of Dogen Zenji, founder of the Soto Zen Buddhist school

"Tractates Cryptica Scriptura" by Philip K. Dick

As part of This Way, scriptural study is not only recommended, but required, as exercising the intellect is seen as a spiritual exercise.

This brief series of questions and answers represents the distillation of the mythical conceptions which form the background of This Way, and essentially summarize our understanding of the spiritual works listed above. Some of the more mythological ideas herein seem quite complex on the surface, but continued perseverance and contemplation will reveal that they are actually fairly straightforward and reasonable, philosophically. Any section herein may safely be bypassed by those frustrated by their complexity. Repeated study, however, should lead the student to a clear understanding.

I: OF THE FIRST CAUSE, THE PLEROMA AND ITS AEONS

Q: What is the nature of the Great Invisible Spirit?

A: The Great Invisible Spirit is called Invisible because it cannot be seen by the eye, nor heard by the ear, nor touched by the hand, nor grasped by the mind of man or God. The Great Invisible Spirit stands behind and beyond nascent Time, manifesting in all possible locations at all possible moments, experiencing all of them simultaneously.

Q: What aspects of the Great Invisible Spirit can be perceived by humans within the World of Forms?

A: Humans can perceive, though darkly and imperfectly, God the Father and Barbelo the Mother, the Great Invisible Spirit's first emanations.

Q: What are the natures of God the Father and Barbelo the Mother?

A: As nothing exists external to the Great Invisible Spirit, its desire to know itself necessitated its achievement of its own knowledge within itself. To do so, it became necessary for the Great Invisible Spirit to divide itself into two separate but equal parts, God the Father, the perceiver, and Barbelo the Mother, the perceived. Together the Father and Mother emanated the Pleroma, Form I, the Kingdom of Heaven and the Aeons therein.

Q: What is the nature of the Pleroma?

A: God the Father and Barbelo the Mother manifested another mask of the Great Invisible Spirit through their emanation of the Piger-Adamas, the Perfect Autogenes, or self-created one. Through knowledge of itself, or its own gnosis, the Autogenes generated within itself five superior Aeons through which to know itself. These five superior Aeons are Pronoia (Forethought), Prognosis (Foreknowledge), Proeido (Foresight), Zoe (Life) and Aphthartos (Incorruptibility). These five superior Aeons also dwell with their five consorts. The consort of Pronoia is Propsyche (Forespirit), the consort of Prognosis is Proskopos (Foredoubt), the consort of Proeido is Teleiosis (Prophecy), the consort of Zoe is Anastasis (Resurrection) and the consort of Aphthartos is Metra (Matrix). Thus do the five Aeons and their consorts allow the Piger-Adamas to know itself through knowledge of God the Father and the Barbelo the Mother.

Q: What is the nature of the Four Luminaries?

A: Through the knowledge of God the Father and Barbelo the Mother and the Autogenes and the Pentad of the Aeons, the One Great Invisible Spirit expressed itself further through the four Luminaries and the Aeons who attended them. The First Luminary is called Armozel, and with Armozel dwell Charis (Grace), Aletheia (Truth) and Morphe (Form). The Second Luminary is called Oroiel, and with Oroiel dwell Katabole (Conception), Aisthesis (Perception) and Mneme (Memory). The Third Luminary is called Davethai, and with Davethai dwell Dianoia (Understanding), Philios (Love) and Idea (Idea). The Fourth Luminary is called Eleleth, and with Eleleth dwell Katartisis (Perfection), Eirene (Peace) and Sophia (Wisdom). These are the Twelve Aeons who sing the knowledge of the Autogenes, and may be discerned by the Knowing Ones through the Mystery of the teachings of the Great Invisible Spirit, manifesting within understanding each time they are expressed and experienced.

Q: What is the great Mystery through which the discerning one might come to discern these Aeons and ascend to the Pleroma?

A: The Mystery of discernment is the Mystery of Ascent.

Q: How did the Aeons and the Luminaries and their Aspects continue to emanate?

A: As the Aeons extended themselves further away from the Great Invisible Spirit, so did the image of God the Father and Barbelo the Mother decrease in their perfection and increase in their qualities, for the greater the number of emanations, the greater the number of qualities found in the Aeons. The Piger-Adamas reflected through the qualities of the Aeons and the Light-bearing

luminaries and their Aspects, giving birth to the One
Hermaphroditic ChristosSophia, the two-in-one Male-
Female whose double aspect is known as Christos and
Sophia. The Christos shares in nature with the Piger-
Adamas, the Nearest Aeon to the Father and Barbelo, and
Sophia with the Farthest emanation who dwells with the
Luminary Eleleth. Thus brought together the
ChristosSophia signify the completion of the Aeons and
the Fullness.

II: OF THE CREATION OF THE WORLD OF FORMS, AND OF THE ARCHONS

Q: What is the World of Forms?

A: The World of Forms is where we reside. It is the
universe which can be perceived by the human via the
physical senses.

Q: How did the World of Forms come to be?

A: In order for it to come to complete knowledge of itself,
the Great Invisible Spirit needed knowledge of
imperfection. For this reason, it comes to pass that Sophia,
desiring to manifest the offspring of the Great Invisible
Spirit, wanted to create without the will of the Father. Her
desire for creation expelled her from the realms of the
Fullness into an emptiness beyond the Pleroma and took
on the aspect of Pistis Sophia. Her error produced an abyss
between the emptiness and the Perfection, like the waters
of the ocean, and the perfection of the Pleroma became as
a reflection underneath those waters, or as a lantern. And
Pistis Sophia ascended forth from the emptiness,

hysterical, knowing that she had erred, yet unaware that her actions were necessary for the gnosis of the Great Invisible Spirit. In Sophia's fall from the Pleroma due to desire, we find echoes of Gautama Buddha's understanding of desire as the root of life's imperfections.

Q: Is the World of Forms consubstantial with the Pleroma?

A: No. The World of Forms is the perishable world, Form II, and is not consubstantial with the imperishable Pleroma.

Q: What is the nature of the offspring of Pistis Sophia?

A: Her offspring, produced without the Gnosis of the Pleroma, took the form of a serpent with the head of a fish. And she called to him, saying, 'Yalda baoth,' which means 'Child, return here.' Blinded by the darkness of the emptiness, this being gazed upon the abyss between the emptiness and the Perfection of the Fullness and believed it was his own reflection, and for this reason he called himself 'Ehyeh,' saying, 'I Am god, and no there are no other gods before me.' This is because he was ignorant of the nature of the Aeons of the Fullness. But, we call him Yaldabaoth, or Saklas, meaning the Blind One, as he is blind to the Fullness, and insane.

Q: What were the actions of the offspring of Pistis Sophia which resulted in the creation of the World of Forms?

A: Believing that he is the Ruler of the Entirety, he took a portion of the Light from his Mother and then moved away from the abyss. Then, after the imperfect image of the Fullness he had seen reflected in the abyss, conceiving of this image as his own thought, he set about creating Authorities with whom he might rule the universe in its many parts. These are the Archons, and their numbers are Twelve and Seventy-Two and Seven and Three-Hundred and Sixty-Five.

Q: What are the names of the Archons?

A: The twelve Archons are named as follows: Athoth, called The Reaper. Harmas, called The Eye of Envy. Kalila-Oumbri. Yabel. Adonaiou, called Sabaoth. Cain. Abel. Abrisene. Yobel. Armoupieel. Melceir-Adonein. Belias.

Q: What is the nature of the Rulers, and how is the World of Forms divided among them?

A: The Archons manifest as follows: Athoth: the Portion of the Ram, Harmas: the Portion of the Bull, Kalila-Oumbri: the Portion of the Twins, Yabel: the Portion of the Crab, Adonaiou Sabaoth: the Portion of the Lion, Cain: the Portion of the Virgin, Abel: the Portion of the Measure, Abrisene: the Portion of the Scorpion, Yobel: the Portion of the Archer, Armoupieel: the Portion of the Goat, Melceir-Adonein: the Portion of the Water Carrier, Belias: the Portion of the Fishes. He then placed five Servitors under each, filling the 72 houses of the Skies. Thus he set about the creation of the skies and the apportioning of the year. And these he placed over the spheres of the Planets. And the Seven Archons are named as follows: Athoth, over the sphere of Saturn; Eloaiou, over the sphere of Jupiter; Astaphaios, over the sphere of Mars; Yao, over the sphere of the Sun; Sabaoth, over the sphere of Venus; Adonin, over the sphere of Mercury; Sabbede, over the sphere of the Moon. Thus he set about the creation of the measure of the week and the qualities of matter. Under each of these Seven he placed 52 Servitors. And each of these Archons truly exists as a duality, as each is apportioned a masculine and feminine aspect.

Q: Is any portion of matter– for instance, that portion which occurs as 'natural' as opposed to 'humans'– consubstantial with the Pleroma?

A: All matter is the World of Forms. Anything that can be perceived with the senses is part of the perishable world which must pass away. For this reason, we also call the World of Forms "the Kenoma," meaning Emptiness.

III. OF THE CREATION OF HUMANKIND, AND THE PRIMARY SALVIFIC EVENT

Q: How did the Archons create humanity?

A: Saklas apportioned among the Authorities a portion of the Light he had stolen from his mother Sophia, and divided the emptiness, establishing an image of the Perfection according to the false impression he had observed. And the Authorities desired to receive praise for their creation, in their arrogance believing themselves the only creators, and believing the Pleroma, reflected in the abyss, their own thoughts. 'Let us create humanity in our image,' they said, and the 365 servitors of the Seven Archons created man and woman from dead matter, and called them Adam and Eve, casting down the image of the Piger-Adamas as Christos and Sophia into base flesh. For this reason, we say that humanity was created in the image of God.

Q: What was the repentance of Sophia?

A: When Sophia realized her mistake, she repented to the Aeons of the Fullness, who forgave with complete forgiveness, as they knew that for the Great Invisible Spirit to attain gnosis of itself, the creation of the realms of emptiness was inevitable and necessary.

Q: How did the Aeons set out to redeem the World of Forms?

A: Sophia, in her great compassion and mercy, desired to rectify her error and redeem her ignorant offspring. God the Father and Barbelo the Mother sent the Christos and Sophia into the realms of matter in order to rend the Waters of the Abyss and allow for the inbreaking of the Pleroma into the World of Forms.

Q: What was the Primary Salvific Event?

A: The Primary Salvific Event was the initial descent of the Christos and Sophia into the World of Forms in order to plant the Spiritual Seed into the first humans. The first humans, created by the Archons, lacked the Spirit granted by the Fullness. In great consternation at their failure to create spiritual beings, the Archons moved back and forth within the emptiness. Descending into the World of Forms through the motion created in the Abyss by the movement of the Archons, Sophia and the Christos carried the Word of the Mind of the Father into the World of Forms. Through the Power of the Word, they spoke to Saklas, urging him as though they were his own thought to grant a portion of the Power he had taken– the Spiritual Seed– into the form of humanity.

Q: What became of the spiritual seed implanted by Sophia and the Christos?

A: Though the first humans held a portion of the Power of the Fullness within themselves, they did not yet have gnosis of the Pleroma. Adam and Eve were placed into a garden in Eden, a paradise created for them by the Archons that they might praise and worship and serve the Archons in their arrogance. Placing the remaining portion of the Power of the Pleroma into a Tree in the center of the Garden, Saklas spoke to the Humans, saying, 'You may eat of any tree of the garden; but of the tree in the center of the Garden you shall not eat, for in if you eat of it you shall taste death.' He said this because he knew that the portion of the Power of the Fullness resided therein, and that if the humans ate of it, they would come to the gnosis of their true natures and usurp the positions of the Archons. The Christos and Sophia, however, descended into the Tree, the Christos taking the form of a Serpent and Sophia the form of a Dove. Appearing thusly, the Christos said to Eve, 'Take of this fruit, and eat, for upon eating this fruit you will come to know your true nature as a part of the Fullness, and will not taste Death.' And Eve took the fruit, and ate of it, giving a portion to Adam.

Q: What is the interpretation of the fruit of gnosis?

A: The interpretation of the fruit of gnosis can be found in the Mystery of the Holy Meal, for as the Christos and Sophia gave a portion of the Power of the Fullness to Eve and Adam, so Eve and Adam partook of the Body and Blood of the Christos in the fruit of the Tree of Gnosis.

Q: What was the result of Adam and Eve's partaking of the fruit of gnosis?

A: After eating of the fruit, Eve and Adam came to know their true natures as containers of the Seed, the Power of the Fullness, and came to understand that they were processors of information created after the form of Piger-Adamas, designed to correct the flaws in the creation of the Archons and know the Great Invisible Spirit so that the Great Invisible Spirit might know itself.

Q: If Adam and Eve came to this understanding upon eating the fruit of the Tree, why does imperfection still exist within the World of Forms?

A: Imperfection exists within this World because the Archons still hold sway over the World of Forms. After Adam and Eve ate of the fruit, the Archons were able to occlude the material aspects of humanity, hiding their memory of the Power of the Fullness deep within their souls.

Q: How were the Archons able to cause this occlusion?

A: This is due to the deficiency of the emptiness in which the World of Forms exists. Coming down over the newly awakened Adam and Eve, the Archons cast them into a deep sleep, buring the Power within their souls and removing them to a Prison constructed of Black Iron, and casting a glamour over their eyes that they considered this Prison like unto the Eden from whence they came. Having reestablished control over Humanity, Saklas instructed them, 'Go forth and multiply, that generations and generations shall worship and praise me, but worship no others, for I am a jealous God.' And this belied his nature as a being of limitation, as if no other deity existed, of whom would he be jealous? And they were fruitful and multiplied, even unto the present time, residing in the Prison of Black Iron under the auspices of the Archons, under the illusion that they yet dwell in the Garden.

IV: OF GNOSIS

Q: What hope is there then for those of us who dwell in the Prison of Iron?

A: Gnosis is our hope and our salvation.

Q: What is gnosis?

A: Gnosis = Awakening (Word + Wisdom). Gnosis must be a deeply personal experience, but not every deeply personal experience is gnosis.

Q: What is Awakening?

A: This might be an epiphany, a theophany, a revelation, etc., but it must be personal and must be experienced.

Q: What is Word?

A: Word is Logos, an informational context into which one can place the awakening event. One of the meanings of Logos is "word," but it also means "faculty of reason," "discourse," "law," "pronouncement." Jesus Christ, as the Logos, represents the deliverer of discourse. Jesus carries forth the Discourse as an extended faculty of reason initiated in the Pleroma by the Divine Seth.

Q: What is the relationship between the Logos and the Christos?

A: The preexistent Logos within the Pleroma is the Christos, which manifests within the World of Forms as living information. He is the instructor who institutes the sacraments– information. He teaches the Way to his disciples– information. He facilitates the presence of the Nous within each of us– information.

Q: Who are the deliverers of the Logos manifested in the World?

A: They are Jesus Christ and Gautama Buddha.

Q: What is Wisdom?

A: The wisdom to apply the awakening event through praxis within one's life. This is our Blessed Mother Sophia, tempered by faith, who carries us forward in our day-to-day existence. She delivers the essential Wisdom necessary to apply the teachings of the Logos to day-to-day life. With her infinite compassion, she descends through the spheres of the Archons to engage the spirit in each of us and allow us to develop compassion for all beings. She allows us to perform the sacraments presented by the Logos wisely, and fills our actions with content, keeping us moving forward and upward as we climb the ladder of emanations towards the realms of the Pleroma.

Q: Is gnosis possible without these three components?

A: No.

Q: Is gnosis different for everyone?

A: No. Although it may *manifest* differently for everyone, it doesn't mean anything anyone wants it to. It is specific to certain contexts.

Q: Can gnosis be achieved via hallucinogens?

A: No. Psychoactive drugs, consisting of matter, are

artifacts of the World of Forms. Artifacts of the World of Forms may assist in personal introspection, but cannot deliver gnosis.

Q: Are there any exceptions to these conditions?

A: Grace is the exception to these conditions. Indeed, the Logos may activate the gnosis of the Pleroma at any time, at any moment. The ways of the Christos and Sophia cannot be truly known by humans, lest the Archons learn of their plans and work against them. Their activities in the World of Forms, and those whom they touch, must remain transparent to the Authorities.

Q: What can we do to cultivate the gnosis of the Fullness within ourselves?

A: Within the limitations of the Black Iron Prison, the person of Knowledge can cultivate the gnosis of the Fullness through the Mysteries established by the Christos and Sophia: Study of, and Devotion to the Word and Living Information, The Ascent Through The Spheres, Mindful Incorporation Into the Continuum of Being.

Q: What is Devotion to the Word and Living Information?

A: Devotion to the Word is sincere and honest study of the Living Information as revealed in history.

Q: What is The Ascent Through The Spheres?

A: The Ascent Through The Spheres is the denial of the Archons and the overcoming of Fate.

Q: What is Mindful Incorporation Into the Continuum of Being?

A: Mindful Incorporation Into the Continuum of Being is the spiritual methodology of the Buddha.

Q: What of the person who has the gnosis of the Christos and Sophia? In what way is this gnosis best expressed?

A: The person who has the gnosis of the Christos and Sophia need only listen to the words of the Holy Valentinus, who says, 'Speak concerning the truth to those who seek it and of knowledge to those who, in their error, have committed sin. Make sure-footed those who stumble and stretch forth your hands to the sick. Nourish the hungry and set at ease those who are troubled. Foster men who love. Raise up and awaken those who sleep.'

V. ON THE NATURE OF HUMANITY AND THE REDEMPTION OF THE WORLD OF FORMS

Q: What is the purpose of humanity?

A: As containers of the Spiritual Seed, which, when activated by the Christos and Sophia, reveals the inbreaking of the Pleroma into the World of Forms, all humans are intrinsically involved with the redemption of the imperfection. This redemption is necessary inasmuch as the completion of the redemption will allow the Great Invisible Spirit to truly Know itself in full knowledge of its emanations. For this reason, the imprisonment must also have occurred, for how can the Great Invisible Spirit come to know itself if it is not first ignorant of some part of itself?

Q: Why has the redemption not already occurred, instantly?

A: The redemption **has** occurred instantly. It is continually occurring. If, indeed, the Great Invisible Spirit is eternal and unchanging, then one cannot limit it in the constraints of Time. The concept of Time is a concept of limitations, and as a concept of limitations, Time is ruled over by the Twelve Archons and Seven Archons and their servitors. Thus, the passage of Time is an illusion maintained within the World of Forms. The process of redemption and of the gnosis of the Great Invisible Spirit has-occurred-is-occurring-will-occur. All that is, that appears of change, is but a single instance, a single firing of a single synapse in the Nous.

Q: What is the nature of humanity?

A: Humankind exists as three-in-one: the hylic, who has surrendered to the Archon, the pneumatic, who has surrendered to the Christos and Sophia, and the psychic, who sometimes surrenders to the Archon, and sometimes to the Christos and Sophia. Those who say that these are three different types of human are in error; for they are but three aspects of all humans, all of whom contain the spiritual seed. The Christos and Sophia can awaken gnosis in any one of these aspects; therefore, it is right and proper for the person of Knowledge to treat all aspects as those who have already had gnosis awakened. Indeed, one can never know where the Christos and Sophia will do their work, for if one could discern this matter with such ease, then the Archons could seek the person out, and put that person to death. Therefore the person of Knowledge will act with compassion, humility, and in service to all of humanity.

Q: What will happen to a person's spirit after the death of the material body if the person dies in a hylic state?

A: One who dies in the state of a hylic aspect has been weighed down by the material, and ensnared by the Archon, and will descend back into a body in the World of Forms according to the control system of the Archons. This does not always mean woe; it does, however, mean rebirth into the realms of limitations and not into the Kingdom of Heaven.

Q: What will happen to a person's spirit after the death of the material body if the person dies in a pneumatic state?

A: The Person of Knowledge dies and is reborn into the Fullness of the Pleroma as soon as the gnosis is realized. After the death of the body, that person ascends into the realms of Perfection, the Fullness, escaping the bonds of the Black Iron Prison and the cycle of incarnation. That spirit, that wonderful and perfected spark of the divine

Light, may also become a Messenger of the Light, taking on a body in the World of Forms out of compassion and mercy for those still trapped within the Prison, along with the Christos and Sophia assisting them with their own resurrections.

Q: What of the Redemption of the World of Forms?

A: The entirety of the World of Forms shall be redeemed that the Great Invisible Spirit might have gnosis of itself, even unto the Archons and Saklas himself. As has been said, 'Not only do humans need redemption, but also the angels, too, need redemption, along with the image and the rest of the Pleromas of the aeons and the wondrous powers of illumination.'

3 FOUR TRUTHS

From these Foundations we can extrapolate Four
Truths, which correlate to the Four Noble Truths of
Gautama Buddha.

1. Life is imperfection.

Every human has the same experience of the
imperfections of life, be they minor inconveniences or
the major struggles of day-to-day existence within
this world, the only position we can state with any
certainty is that perfection is an impossibility within
the World of Forms.

**2. The origin of imperfection is separation from the
Fullness of the Pleroma.**

And yet, there is a place of perfection– The Fullness,
or Pleroma. Our separation from the Fullness into the

World of Forms resulting from God's desire to know itself causes this apparent imperfection. We are ignorant of the Pleroma, and this causes us to believe that other sentient beings are in no way connected to us, and that the sensations we experience are unrelated to one another.

3. It is possible to reconnect to the Pleroma.

There is an accessible seed of divinity within each one of us. Developing knowledge of that spark– gnosis– creates an abiding insight into the nature of one's self. This allows one to reconnect to the fullness of the Pleroma and escape the endless cycle of birth and death.

4. Reconnection to the Pleroma is possible via this Way, the cultivation of gnosis.

This Way is moving from the Kenomic Worldview– the worldview of Emptiness– to the Pleromic Worldview– the worldview of Fullness. Another way to say this is that the primary goal of a Way person is to reduce suffering, both for one's self and for others, through self-knowledge and mindfulness. This can be achieved through the cultivation of gnosis.

Gnosis is a state of insight brought about by the application of living information and wisdom to an

awakening experience. Or, to put it another way,
Gnosis = Awakening (Word + Wisdom).

4 MOVING FROM EMPTINESS TO FULLNESS

What do the Four Truths and the Foundations really mean within the context of day-to-day existence within the World of Forms? They present a road map with which we can move from the Kenoma to the Pleroma. As above, so below. The redemption of the imperfect World of Forms takes place on two levels, Macro- and Microcosmic. The processes mirror one another; what is happening to the Kosmos at large is also happening to each and every individual. If one drafted a ontological map of the Kosmos and laid it over an ontological map of an individual, they'd be exceptionally similar.

The process happens in two "Worlds" or realms: the Kenomic and the Pleromic. The Kenomic realm is characterized by emptiness, existential ennui, a lack of purpose, imperfection. This lack of purpose manifests as adherence to the idea of Fate or

Determinism. The Pleromic realm (the Kingdom of Heaven) is characterized by fulfillment, a sense of teleological well-being. This sense of purpose manifests as Self-Individuation or Confidence. This is why when we move to the Pleromic realm we're said to have been freed from Fate and Determinism.

The Kenomic Worldview, the default human condition here in the World of Forms, is marked by a deeply embedded sense of existential ennui, manifested especially as a sense of purposelessness. The Greek term "kenoma," emptiness or void, was used by some Gnostics to describe the World in which we reside. Its opposite is "pleroma," or spiritual fullness.

The emptiness which contrasts with the fullness of the Pleromic Worldview resides under layers of what Philip K. Dick called "kipple"-- meaningless content-- but is not always completely manifested (for the manifestation of utter emptiness would annihilate an individual). Rather, it appears like something submerged off the shore of a great lake of extraneous stuff, visible when the tide recedes and vanishing when the tide increases, but always there below the surface.

The problem with approaches to the Kenomic

Worldview in many circles is its equation to emotions or thoughts, the false heart/brain dichotomy. One equates the Kenomic Worldview with sadness, or dissatisfaction, or depression, or with entrapment by material distractions. This approach confuses the kipple with the Worldview itself. One can be perfectly happy or in love or extremely wealthy and still dwell within the Kenoma. One can also be melancholy or sad or angry or poor and still dwell within the Pleroma.

If you live in the Kenomic World, you have no idea what you're doing here. You may have a relatively happy life by your culture's standards. Nonetheless, the basic routines of life seem meaningless and trite. You likely get up each morning, eat breakfast, drink some coffee, take out the dog, take a shower and head to work. You do your job, perhaps happily–– it may even be a job you enjoy very much! You go home to your family, with whom you are deeply in love, watch some television and hit the hay. Or, perhaps you wake up in the morning, do some Yoga, go for a quick jog and shower, eat a healthy breakfast. Then you go to your job at an eco-friendly Ad firm that caters to progressive political causes. You head home, read for a while and meditate, do some gardening and then hit the hay. Nonetheless, in any or all of these cases, a feeling of emptiness and purposelessness abides.

In the Kenoma, you are subject to Fate. You convince yourself that you have to do what you're doing because of the influence of external powers (the need for food, shelter, etc.). Horoscopes work for you, as do other divinatory systems like weathermen or work schedules, all of which predict possible futures only inasmuch as you provide them with import. When these divinatory devices fail to produce the expected results, you become frustrated.

You do what you do because you have to do it, whether that thing is going to your job at a corporation or chanting to the Buddha of Compassion or praying the Rosary. You're fated to do these things, and stuck in a situation from which you can't escape.

You may try to suppress the emptiness with externalities, purchases, mind-altering substances or abstract busy-ness. Conversely, you may try to fill the emptiness with good works and "positive" thoughts, with Spiritual Practice or Love, with meditation or Prayer. You will find, however, again and again, that none of these approaches work to finally rid yourself of the empty feeling from which the Kenomic

Worldview develops.

Why does the Kenomic Worldview develop in so many? It is because, macrocosmically, those of us who dwell in the Kenoma were born into the World of Forms, under the control of the Demiurge and the Archons. As Jesus says in the Gospel of Thomas, a little child seven days old is closer to the Kingdom of Heaven than an old man. As we grow older within a milieu in which we are taught that we have very little control of the external world, the Archons work to cover us in layers and layers of kipple. This goes beyond the usual platitudes about social "conformity" and politics and the value of public education; these are all externalities which, though they may be important, must take a back seat if one is working to move from the Kenomic World to the Pleromic.

The Kenomic individual all too frequently points the finger outside of him/herself when addressing the hollowness inside. This is the individual who risks falling into what we call "the Anarchonic Fallacy," the erroneous trope that salvation comes through rebellion. This fallacious condition maintains that the emptiness within develops as a result of the "Parents" or "Church" or "Science" or "Politics." Although the Kenoma is reflected and contained within each of these things to the extent that it is reflected and contained within individuals, railing against them is in and of itself an Archonic act, an error of collectivist irrationality, judging an entire body of persons based upon what may be a single aspect of a single individual one has encountered. Transcending the Kenoma doesn't entail becoming a "nonconformist" or fighting against perceived "injustices" or religio-political organizations or any other external thing. Working to fight against social injustices is always a good thing, but one can do so and still dwell within the Kenoma.

Thankfully, we each have a spark of the Pleromic World within us. Clement of Alexandria quotes the "Prophetic Scriptures" as saying, "As to gnosis, some elements of it we already possess; others, by what we do possess, we firmly hope to attain. For neither have we attained all, nor do we lack all." In essence, gnosis exists to allow an individual to create a teleology, to defend their own self-worth, to uncover a reason for being. The achievement of gnosis via the Logos and Sophia enables one to perceive the Pleromic purpose, or reason for being. Although this will not completely eliminate the Kenomic Condition, it will at least provide blueprints with which the Gnostic can begin constructing a ladder to the Pleromic realms.

Not everyone needs to know their reason for

being, and this is fine. Only those who do, who are
driven to seek the Pleroma, are invited to leave the
Kenomic World, to accept the outstretched hands of
the Logos and Sophia and rise above the bottomless
pit of the Kenoma.

The Pleromic Worldview, the goal of this Way,
manifests as a sense and knowledge of purpose and
spiritual fullness in the face of the imperfection of the
World of Forms. In the Pleromic individual, body,
soul and spirit are aligned with the Aeons, or higher
aspects of the self, as a manifestation of the perfected
human. In contrast to the Kenomic person, whose
actions and life seem aimless and listless, the Pleromic
person has a heightened sense of purpose. This
certainty may not be discernible or recognizable; it
may dwell beneath the surface of one's day-to-day
activities. As the hallmark of the Pleroma is shared
experience, the sense of purpose of the Pleromic
person never materializes as megalomaniacism or
egocentricity. There is never a need to "take over the
world" or become material successful in the physical
realm. The Pleromic Worldview decreases, instead of
increases, a need for power of any kind.

Although unable to completely escape the
vagaries of the material world or the tyranny of
inanimate objects, the person who lives in the

Pleromic World has a heightened sense of awareness of the consequences of his or her actions. Whereas within the Kenomic World one is subject to a singular Fate, the Pleromic individual's "time sense" expands, allowing him or her to interact with causation and assess the effects of motions within the space/time stream. This allows the Pleromic person to interact with others and the World of Forms fearlessly but cautiously. Pleromic individuals often seem "psychic" or prodigious, somehow more intelligent or wise, but this is the result of the expanded time sense and the projection of potentialities into the atmosphere of the World of Forms.

The earmark of the Pleromic individual is not happiness, but dignity, confidence and tranquility (*ataraxia*). You may be depressed and miserable with your circumstances in the World of Forms, but underneath you understand and know that the Good exists, that the Present is temporary and eternal, and— more importantly— what these things mean and how they effect your lifestyle. You carry yourself with a healthy posture, respectful of, and interested in, the experiences you have. The Pleromic Worldview can just as readily manifest as what appears to be foolishness or childishness, but this is rare, and dignity is maintained.

As the Kenomic individual often attempts to ameliorate his or her emptiness by devaluing others, the Pleromic individual is far more likely to give others the benefit of the doubt in almost every case. This does not mean that you fall prey to the vapid blustering of sentimentality, but that you recognize the inherent worth of every individual and the futility of argument when one has become intimate with the Pleroma. The Pleromic individual refuses to identify other individuals as valueless objects.

Thoughts and feelings are not the roots of the Pleromic Worldview; rather, they are extensions thereof. You can have a "poor attitude" towards something within the Pleroma just as easily as you can have a great outlook in the Kenoma. You can have negative thoughts about something within the Pleroma just as easily as you can believe in the "Power of Positive Thinking" in the Kenoma. In the Pleroma, however, you understand the consequences of your attitude and your thoughts.

Why do we not exist within the Pleromic World from the get-go? One could certainly argue that we do, that as a child you are born into the Pleroma but the World of Forms and Fate drape the folds of the

Kenoma over you as you grow and learn and interact with the World and the Archons. Nonetheless, it is through the application of the Logos, or Word and Sophia, or Wisdom, that one transforms the dross of the Kenoma into the shining splendor of the Pleroma.

Due to the nature of the World of Forms, Pleromic individuals are few and far between. Just as no one who dwells in the World of Forms dwells completely in the Kenoma due to the presence of the Divine Spark within each of us, so no one who dwells in the World of Forms dwells completely in the Pleroma as we dwell within the realm of Imperfection and Images. Nonetheless, as multiple instances of a singular consciousness which is experiencing itself through all of its aspects, we have a responsibility, if so called, to seek the life of the Pleroma at all costs, whenever and wherever possible.

Every person has his or her foot in both realms, but usually one more than the other (and usually the Kenomic more than the Pleromic). Just as only the individual really knows what happens during 'gnosis,' only the individual can decide what realm he or she lives in. You can't point to someone and say "You're Kenomic!" because you can only make that assessment for yourself. Nonetheless, everybody who's walking around falls somewhere on this spectrum between emptiness and a total sense of purpose.

The Kenomic and Pleromic states are independent of mythology, and can't be induced by another person. For some people, it will never even be an issue, and this is okay; **This Way is not for people who are happy and contented and already have a sense of purpose– it's for people who are living in the Kenomic world.** This is what the moral admonition means in the *Gospel of Truth*:

> Speak concerning the truth to those who seek it and of knowledge to those who, in their error, have committed sin. Make sure-footed those who stumble and stretch forth your hands to the sick. Nourish the hungry and set at ease those who are troubled. Foster men who love. Raise up and awaken those who sleep. For you are this understanding which encourages. If the strong follow this course, they are even stronger. Turn your attention to yourselves. Do not be concerned with other things, namely, that which you have cast forth from yourselves, that which you have dismissed. Do not return to them to eat them. Do not be moth-eaten. Do not be worm-eaten, for you have already shaken it off. Do not be a place of the devil, for you have already destroyed him. Do not strengthen your last obstacles, because that is reprehensible. For the lawless one is nothing. He harms himself more than the law. For that one does his works because he is a lawless person. But this one, because he is a righteous person, does his works

among others. Do the will of the Father, then, for you are from him.

Gnosis is what transforms the Kenomic realm into the Pleromic realm on both levels. For gnosis to happen, one needs both the **Logos**– Reason/Word– and **Sophia**– Wisdom. Where do these originate, and by what are the processed? **Nous**– Mind. Barbelo– the most comprehensible expression of the Great, Androgynous, Incomprehensible Invisible Spirit– injected the Christos into the World of Forms from the Pleromic world, where it became the Logos, which is activated by the Sophianic power that is already present in the Kenoma.

The Logos is *Reasoned Information*: scriptures, rites, rituals, myths, literally **stuff that can be communicated with words**.[5] Sophia is our inner capacity to comprehend the Logos– this is why you need both. Every time someone in the Kenomic realm is exposed to the Logos, they have the opportunity to achieve gnosis provided they have also embraced Sophia. This is why so many people can read all this stuff and do all these rites and not have any real progress– too much focus but no way to apply it. On the other hand, if one embraces Sophia

---

[5] Not the words themselves-- an important distinction!

but neglects the Logos, one is simply spinning one's wheels in place. This is why so many New Agers and Buffet-spirituality types can't nail it down– *they won't pick something to do*– all kinds of stuff to *apply*, but no words to *focus on*.

The perfect resident of the Pleromic World is the Autogenes, or self-generated. The Autogenes generates itself, but is also the state of being that the Gnostic creates for him or herself– "self-generated" and "self, generated." The Autogenes stands "above" the Aeons because it is comprised of the Aeons– it is the synergistic summation of all of the Aeons, which are the 'positive' Ideals that comprise the Autogenes– peace, perfection, beauty, wisdom, etc. When one of these Aeons– Sophia– refuses to comprehend its own attachment to the source, it creates a bastard, the Demiurge. Microcosmically, this means that one's Wisdom, when applied for selfish reasons (i.e. without consideration of the holistic nature of the Kosmos) creates Ego. Ego then transforms the Aeons– perfection, peace, love, etc.– into Archons– fear, power, lust, etc.

The idea of the self-as-realized is the Autogenes. The idea of self-without-realization is the Counterfeit Spirit. One can literally "contact" the Autogenes by writing a list of everything one wants from one's life, and all of the qualities one wants to realize– these are the Aeons. In the same way, by listing everything one hates about one's self, or all of the qualities one has that one wants to abandon, one can "contact" one's Counterfeit Spirit (Doppelganger).

The Autogenes is the Divine Twin of the human being, that into which one must transform one's self. To move from the Kenomic world to the Pleromic world, the Archons need to be redeemed and transformed into Aeons. How do we do this? There are various ways; for instance, this is what the whole Ascent Prayer tradition is all about (Jeu, Allogenes, etc.). Each Archon is considered, faced, and bypassed in order to transform it into its Aeonic "mirror image." When this has happened, the human and the twin merge (like Jesus and his Twin in the Pistis Sophia), and one enters the realm of the Pleroma.

Almost nobody can move completely from the Kenomic Realm to the Pleromic Realm in one's lifetime. In the same way, almost nobody is ever 100% Kenomic or Pleromic (the people who are usually change the world). When the balance moves from the Kenomic to the Pleromic in enough individuals *who do so of their own volition*, that's when the Kingdom of Heaven manifests and everything is perfected. This is why when we move from the Kenoma to the Pleroma, we won't "taste death."[6]

---

[6] See *The Gospel of Thomas,* Saying 1

5 GNOSIS IS THE SAME FOR EVERYONE

There's a pervasive misunderstanding about gnosis in the modern world; a meme exists which says that "gnosis is different for everyone," that everyone's experience of gnosis is different and that gnosis is a malleable state, devoid of ontological substance. This is Relativist Gnosis, and it's incorrect. It's based on a poorly autodidactic New Age understanding of "gnosis," which shares very little with the idea as understood in the Nag Hammadi texts.[7] "Gnosis is different for everyone" is the rallying cry of the spiritually self-indulgent who have one neat-o experience and consider themselves enlightened masters.

In reality, however, the experience of gnosis is

---

[7] See Jesse Folks' "Self-Definition as What is Rejected Rather Than What is Affirmed," http://goo.gl/zUNeC

the same for everyone who has it. Gnosis is Objective Truth. It is a cultivated experience derived from the inbreaking of the Pleroma, or True Reality, into the World of Forms, or Illusion. As an experience of Truth, it is the exact same experience for everyone. If the experience were relative, it wouldn't be Truth, and if it wasn't Truth, it couldn't be gnosis.

Now, here's the rub: *objectivity appears as subjectivity when filtered through the lens of existence in the World of Forms*. Our *experiences* of gnosis **must** be identical. However, as we are trapped in this World of Limitations, our *ability to describe this experience* must also be limited. These descriptions are what makes gnosis *seem* subjective, or different from person to person. "Everyone has his or her own gnosis" is false. The correct statement should be, "everyone has his or her own description of gnosis." It's a subtle distinction, but very important.

There is the Experiencer (the Spiritual Seed– Humanity) which is trapped within the World of Forms. Then, there is the Experienced– Truth, or The Father, or The Limitless Light or what have you. Gnosis is the intersection of the two, a combination of the Logos, or Word, and Sophia, or Wisdom, and Epiphany, or Awakening.

Now, the *Gospel of Philip* says that, "Truth did not come into the world naked, but it came in types and images." The only possible way Truth can be expressed in the World, by itself or by others, is in "types and images"– imperfect copies of itself. However, it also says (emph. mine) that "....Truth brought names into existence in the world for our sakes, because it is not possible to learn it (truth) without these names. *Truth is one single thing*; it is many things and for our sakes to teach about this one thing in love through many things." As gnosis is the perception of this "one single thing," gnosis requires the "many things" described above — Logos, Sophia, Awakening– to truly be Gnosis. And, these "many things" may take different external forms, but internally, the connection between the Experiencer and the Experienced **must** be identical for anyone who has the experience.

So, the worldly information that contains and expresses gnosis may have some variation, but the experience underneath this containment and expression is the same. The textual evidence may be different– *On the Origin of the World* versus *The Gospel of Truth*, say — but the experiences of gnosis underlying these texts is identical. A drop of wine is different than a chalice full, but both are still 80%

water, 13% ethanol and 7% other stuff.

We might describe what happened to us during
an epiphanic event. We may create myths or
participate in rituals designed as an attempt to
communicate this indescribable Knowledge. The
Knowledge itself, however, exists **behind** the
epiphany, the rituals and the myths, and if it is not
the same for each of us, we have nothing that binds
us to the Truth.

A dog, a cat, a mouse, a cow and a donkey, all
starving, commiserated together in a stable during a
time of famine. The dog said, "Our problem is that
we have no meat to eat." The cat shook his head, and
answered, "foolish dog. Obviously we suffer due to a
lack of fish." "You are both incorrect," said the mouse,
"as cheese is the solution to our misery." "Not cheese,
but grass, would make us happiest," mooed the cow.
"Stupid animals," thought the donkey. "None of them
realize that we would all be better off with piles and
piles of delicious oats."

6 POROSIS: THE OPPOSITE OF GNOSIS

Although one might think that the opposite of gnosis would be *agnosis*, or ignorance, the Way finds its opposite in the quality of *porosis*, a term meaning hardness of heart, dullness, lacking in mental acuity. We find this term used in scripture in a number of places. In Mark's Gospel, Chapter 3, for instance, Jesus is challenged in the synagogue by those present for desiring to heal the withered hand of a man on the Sabbath (emphasis mine in all following examples):

> And he asked them, "Is it lawful to do good on the
> Sabbath, or to do evil? To save life, or to kill?" But
> they wouldn't answer him. And when he'd looked
> around in anger at them, distressed at *the hardness of*
> *their hearts*, he said to the man, "Stretch forth your
> hand." And he stretched it out, and his hand was

made as whole as the other.

In the Epistle to the Ephesians, the Apostle Paul uses
the term once again while delivering advice on
Christian living to those people:

> Now this I say and testify in the Lord, that you must
> no longer walk as the Gentiles do, in the futility of
> their minds. They are darkened in their
> understanding, alienated from the life of God because
> of the ignorance that is in them, due to their *hardness*
> *of heart.*

In the Sethian literature, we find the same phrase
used in the text *Authoritative Teaching*, this time to
describe those Servants of the Archons who assail the
soul:

> But these – the ones who are ignorant – do not seek
> after God. Nor do they inquire about their dwelling-
> place, which exists in rest, but they go about in
> bestiality. They are more wicked than the pagans,
> because first of all they do not inquire about God, for
> *their hardness of heart* draws them down to make them
> their cruelty. Furthermore, if they find someone else

who asks about his salvation, *their hardness of heart*
sets to work upon that man. And if he does not stop
asking, they kill him by their cruelty, thinking that
they have done a good thing for themselves.

Indeed they are sons of the devil! For even pagans
give charity, and they know that God who is in the
heavens exists, the Father of the universe, exalted over
their idols, which they worship. But they have not
heard the word, that they should inquire about his
ways. Thus the senseless man hears the call, but he is
ignorant of the place to which he has been called.
And he did not ask during the preaching, "Where is
the temple into which I should go and worship my
hope?"

On account of his senselessness, then, he is worse
than a pagan, for the pagans know the way to go to
their stone temple, which will perish, and they
worship their idol, while their hearts are set on it
because it is their hope. But to this senseless man the
word has been preached, teaching him, "Seek and
inquire about the ways you should go, since there is

nothing else that is as good as this thing." The result is that the substance of *hardness of heart* strikes a blow upon his mind, along with the force of ignorance and the demon of error. They do not allow his mind to rise up, because he was wearying himself in seeking that he might learn about his hope.

In the *Secret Book of John*, this quality is given to those who do not participate in the story:

And thus the whole creation became enslaved forever, from the foundation of the world until now. And they took women and begot children out of the darkness according to the likeness of their spirit. *And they closed their hearts, and they hardened themselves through the hardness of the counterfeit spirit until now.*

According to our Way, Gnosis = Awakening (Word + Wisdom). As such, we may define Porosis as **Unconsciousness (Willful Ignorance + Willful Selfishness)**.

Unconsciousness is, of course, the natural state of an individual trapped in the World of Forms. It is the unawakened state, the state prior to epiphany or theophany or enlightenment or samadhi or what have you.

Willful Ignorance occurs when one has been presented with the Word, but for whatever reason chooses not just to ignore it, but to oppose it. Obviously those who have never been exposed to the Word cannot be charged with being Willfully Ignorant, which is one of the essential reasons that Ignorance itself cannot be the opposite of gnosis. We find Willful Ignorance in the character of the Demiurge, who, presented with the revelation that he is not the True God, nonetheless carries on as though he is.

Willful Selfishness is, of course, the quality of willfully placing one's self-satisfaction or pride at a place of supreme importance. We find Willful Selfishness in the character of Pistis Sophia, who, by desiring to create without first returning to the Limitless Light, brings the World of Forms into being.

As gnosis is the earmark of the Pleromic Worldview, so Porosis describes the state of the individual most firmly involved in the Kenomic Worldview. Neither of these states are static; there is no perfected gnosis within the World of Forms, nor is there a perfected Porosis. Gnosis is something to be cultivated and typically manifests as a temporary state; Porosis also manifests as a temporary state brought about by the intersection of the three qualities of which it consists. Porosis is as drastic as gnosis, but in the other direction.

It is primarily designed as a tool to help the rational Way person to avoid falling into such a state. With the definition of this quality in mind, we can ask ourselves, am I being Willfully Ignorant or Selfish? Am I acting as a Pleromic individual, or as someone inside of the Kenoma? We can attempt to avoid Porosis within ourselves, but we must always hesitate before using this tool to evaluate others.

Jeremy Puma

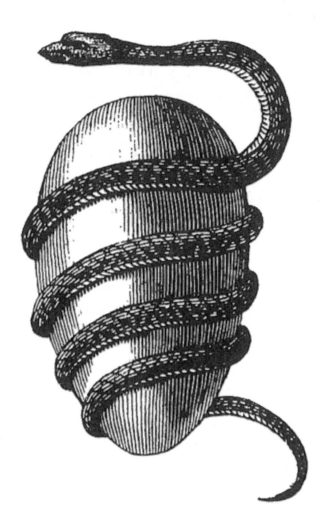

PART II: PRACTICE

7 WORD: **THE GATE OF THE NOUS**

In New Age circles, much claptrap gets produced about the so-called superiority of the "Knowledge of the Heart." The idea is so prevalent that it has even leaked into the mainstream. You'll be talking about spirituality with somebody and they'll say "well what we think is stupid/unimportant. It's what we *feel in the heart* that's important." Or they'll go on about how the mind is somehow masculine and therefore patriarchal and domineering but the heart is somehow feminine and therefore matriarchal and *better than you are.*

All of this heart-versus-mind talk is nonsense. It's the Nietzschean understanding of Apollo versus Dionysus put through the wringer of postmodern feminist radicalism and spewed out into society via the New Age movement. It's Oprah and the ladies from The View sitting around and nodding sagely while some namby-pamby shill spits out the latest platitudes about "being true to your Inner Truth" and "exercising compassionate compassion." It's also militant atheists Richard Dawkins and Christoper

Hitchens telling a little old Catholic lady that she's a dumb idiot for saying her novena. It's endemic, and epidemic, and it has to stop.

This division between the Mind and the Heart is a very recent phenomenon, historically speaking, and has to do with the conflation of the *Mind* with the *brain*. In ancient Mediterranean cultures, the physical heart was actually the part of the body that did the thinking; it was the seat of the Rational Soul. The brain, on the other hand, was essentially thought to exist to fill in the big hole in the middle of the skull (why do you think the Egyptians composted the brain when they mummified someone?).[8]

The Mind, on the other hand, was the Divine Nous, nous being the word for mind.[9] It was the transcendent quality that granted Reason to the earnest seeker, the producer of the Forethought of God. Plato considered the "Noetic" level the highest level of abstraction or Ideal attainable by humans, which was experienced through an abstract concept termed noesis. Lower levels of abstraction (more physical sensations) were only experienced through *episteme*, indirect knowledge. To Plato, art and gnosis were perefectly compatible as art was a function of

---

[8] Nunn, John Francis. *Ancient Egyptian Medicine.*

[9] For an excellent treatment of the noos as an organ, see *The Early Greek Concept of the Soul* by Jan N. Bremmer.

Nous, whereas one who only had episteme wasn't really in tune with Mind and therefore not a good candidate for the Sorbonne.

The Egyptian Hermetists-- very influenced by Platonism-- understood the Nous as the highest seat of Divine Reason, and mortal reasoning found in the heart reflected this superior mentation. The Rational Soul of the heart processed sensations and perceptions collected by sensation, which were then given internal Form and Structure through the medium of the Nous. Mentation and intellectual exercise provided noesis of the Nous, and these exercises weren't considered in light of some heart/brain dichotomy. In other words, it wasn't "organic brain thinks, organic heart feels" in the ancient world, it was "Rational Soul seated in the heart processes experience, Nous/noesis perfects experience."

The dichotomy between heart and mind came about when the brain was recognized as the organ that thinks, a gradual process that played out over thousands of years. By the time of the Age of Reason, Descartes and other philosophers began to understand the brain as the sole seat of Reason or mentation, and as Reason was venerated, so episteme became its sole endeavour. As Science marched onwards, exceptional importance was placed on the Brain as the seat of reason, and the Intellect was seen as the be-all, end-all of experience. This ill-fated point of view gave birth to imperialism and atheism, and Western culture developed a superiority complex based on their mastery of episteme as opposed to noesis. The pinnacle of the lionizing of the brain gave birth to such movements as The Science of Mind churches and, most notably, scientific psychology, which, while absolutely integral as a practical philosophy, overwhelmingly (with some exceptions like Jung) demoted noetic experience, classifying it as either a symptom of mental illness or a product of a disjointed episteme.

This Age of Enlightenment, while certainly notable for the contributions it made to the realm of episteme, confused the Dickens out of Nous and the brain. Even occultism was approached as a "science" by the likes of H. P. Blavatsky, who unwittingly confined it to the realms of the brain, to episteme instead of noesis. Blavatsky even supported the theories of "racial evolution," creating what was actually a kind of "spiritual materialism" consisting of pointless epistemologies like "Planetary Evolution" and "Racial Evolution" and the asinine theory that apes are the decendants of humans, and not vice-versa.[10] Theosophy's problem has never been its veracity (or lack thereof), it's always been its desire to turn wildly speculative supposition into concrete, measurable theories via a pseudo-scientific approach.

---

[10] See "A Walker or a Climber" in Blavatsky's *The Secret Doctrine.*

Eventually, the pseudo-enlightenment of the mid-Twentieth Century attempted to compensate for this worship of the brain by swinging in an entirely different direction. Scholars of culture and spirituality began to rebel against the overwhelmingly epistemological current that had been most culturally prevalent for so long, but in their desire to rectify the perceived wrongs of centuries, simply flipped the coin to its other side. Now the heart, the feminine, the emotional and irrational became the measuring stick by which experience was measured and perfected. Anti-intellectualism, a trait shared both by fascist regimes and anti-scholastic spiritualists who oppose "book learning," ran rampant. In short, by rebelling against the brain, these movements damaged our connection to the Mind.

Anti-intellectualism is still incredibly prevalent in all manner of mystical traditions, though usually under the banner of anti-*episteme*. Why read books when you can take ayahuasca? Why go to school to learn about something when people who never went to school can teach you just as well? Why do we need the connection to Nous provided by the Christos when the Comfort of Sophia will do just fine? After all, isn't gnosis different for everyone, and isn't it all about *personal experience*?

This all, however, confuses the issue, because it's all based on a false premise, that the mind and heart are seperate because the brain "thinks" and the heart "feels." In reality, as the Hermetists knew, there is no distinction between heart and mind, no knowledge of one that is superior to the knowledge of another. The equation is actually rather simple: the Rational Soul processes as it collects, the Nous processes and perfects.

According to This Way, the universe consists of living information which is collected by the Rational Soul through the medium of the heart and the brain. As it collects this information, it processes it, and if one has the connection to the Nous, this information is passed along to God. It may help to think of this in terms of a two-way radio. The Rational Soul is the dial, and when it's properly tuned, it receives communication from the waves of information produced by the universe. When activated by the information that is alive, it achieves gnosis and a connection is made between the individual and the Nous, which broadcasts that information.

There is a strong pro-mentation current running through various Nag Hammadi traditions, most notably those traditions that produced texts like Allogenes, Marsanes and The Books of the Saviour (Pistis Sophia). As pointed out to the author by Jesse Folks, a student of ancient Christianity and its facets:

> The "original sin" (IE the error that caused the fall) in gnostic myth is Sophia's attempt to comprehend the Godhead without her rational, masculine counterpart. Her attempt at understanding God via intuitive emotional

faculties is why we have misery, suffering, evil, and materiality. That's a pretty strong statement that being "feely" untempered by "thinky" was considered to be a very, very bad thing by the authors behind the myths. This story "humanizes" Sophia in a sense and thus becomes a potent parable for understanding ourselves and our own motives for questing after the divine in various ways. But the root of the primordial tragedy is pretty clear: being "feely" is pretty much worthless if you can't balance it with "thinky."[11]

This current-- the reification of Reason-- is one that many have been loathe to embrace because the Sophianic current has been so overwhelming in its need for compensation that the idea of mentation as a spiritual path has taken a back seat to the pure emotion and feeling of ritual. If one is at all interested in practical spirituality, however, one must respect the fact that intellectual practice is just as pertinent to that path-- in some ways even moreso-- because *it is through intellectual pursuits that the information contained in our universe becomes Living Information.*

The person with a connection to Nous participates in practice by reviving the Word, bringing that which is dead (ancient knowledge, for instance) back to life. Writing a book, or reading a

---

[11] http://goo.gl/bNe8s

scripture, can be spiritual practices. The ancient Egyptian scribes were religious figures, and the Alexandrian Hermetists considered the act of writing sacred (thus the whole Hermes/Thoth connection). We should be venerating the intellect as equal to emotion, not something in opposition to it. The Christos and Sophia are bride and groom and brother and sister, not master and servant or servant and master. That Mary Magdalene may or may not have been Jesus's number one apostle doesn't mean that the mind is somehow inferior to the heart, but this is the kind of extrapolation we see in our confused society more and more these days.

Study! Read! Think! Reason! Embrace the Mind, and come closer to the Nous through the medium of the Logos. This Way is impossible without so doing.

8 +WISDOM: **FOUR VIRTUES AND THE PRECEPTS**

The practice of This Way continues with focusing on the Four Virtues of Wisdom.

The First Virtue, **Inquiry,** is the act of asking questions, the first step on any path, which must never be abandoned if one wishes to experience gnosis. Inquiry is a methodology that can be applied to any endeavor. This act allows for answers and conclusions, but only after all aspects of the question have been pursued. Questions concerning worldly things must be asked from the perspective of one expecting no definitive conclusion. One must not seek to question individual aspects of an epistemological framework but the framework in its entirety. For instance, we might ask which political theory is best for society but it is better that we ask whether "political theory" or "society" are valid constructions in and of themselves. The keywords of the first Virtue are *skepticism, cynicism, stoicism.*

The Second Virtue, **Compassion**, is the root of Love, based on an understanding of the self as one with the other. As we are all containers of sparks of the divine, all part of the Limitless Light, so what we do to the least of us we do to ourselves. Let the Solitary represent the Lowest Common Denominator in the sense that we recognize the common bond of divinity present in all persons, down to the very least of us. Gnosis is impossible without compassion for the lowest of the low, the God manifesting in the trash strata (as says Philip Dick: "The symbols of the divine show up in our world initially at the trash stratum").

The Third Virtue, **Humility**, is the natural result of Compassion and admittance that our experience in the World of Forms is imperfect and subjective. It is the realization that we are exceptionally limited in physical range and abilities. For instance, we get sick and die. We suffer from all the realities of finitude.

The Fourth Virtue, **Service**, is the cornerstone of the virtues and expresses the fact that we cultivate a desire to serve others. Through inquiry, compassion and humility, we arrive at a desire to alleviate the sorrows of other beings trapped within the World of

Forms, whatever those sorrows may be. We understand, through gnosis, that with the alleviation of the suffering of other conscious beings we also alleviate our own suffering. Indeed, we even alleviate the suffering of the wounded universe.

When one has an understanding of the Four Virtues, one may consider the following precepts as guideposts along the Way. Perfect adherence to the precepts is unnecessary-- impossible, even-- while in the World of Forms; however, they can assist one's transition from the Kenomic Worldview to that of the Pleroma.

The Major Precepts of This Way: Renunciation of the Archons

The Major Precepts are intended for anyone interested in This Way.

I will earnestly and honestly endeavour to renounce the words and deeds of:

Illusion (Athoth).

Ignorance (Eloaiou).

Lust (Astaphaios).

Power (Yao).

Violence (Sabaoth).

Folly (Adonin).

Anger (Sabbade).

The Lesser Precepts of This Way, from the *Third Book of the Saviour* (also called *Pistis Sophia*):

The Lesser Precepts are intended for those who choose to intensively practice this Way.

I will earnestly and honestly endeavour to renounce:

...hatred of the body, and love of the body.
...gossip and idle talk.
...eavesdropping.
...litigiousness.
...slander.
...false witness.
...pride.
...lust.
...theft.
...wickedness.
...pitilessness.
...wrath.
...cursing.
...strife.

…ignorance.

…adultery.

…murder.

…sloth.

…atheism.

…fortune telling and low magic [see note that follows].

…blasphemy.

I will earnestly and honestly endeavour to practice:

…patience.

…calmness.

…loving-kindness.

…gentleness.

…peacefulness.

…mercy.

…charity.

…service.

…piety.

…righteousness.

…goodness.

Escaping Astral Determinism

The Lesser Precepts of the Way proscribe the practice of fortune telling. The Way person places no value in the casting of horoscopes or attempts to discern future events via divination, scrying, low magic, etc. There are both mythic and practical reasons for this point of view.

Mythically, the Sethians were very concerned with what we refer to as "escaping astral determinism." This is the idea of escaping from "*heimarmene*," or fate, by recognizing and denying the influence of the astrological Archons on one's existence in the World of Forms. In the Books of the Saviour (Pistis Sophia), we find entire passages which discuss the Christos' ascent through the Planetary Spheres, during which he "changes the direction" of the Spheres, thereby ruining the ability of astrologers to divine:

> ...[T]hou hast taken their power from them and from their horoscope-casters and their consulters and from those who declare to the men in the world all things which shall come to pass, in order that they should no more from this hour know how to declare unto them any thing at all which will come to pass.[12]

At a later point in the codice, in a different book in

---

[12] Mead, G.R.S. trans. *Pistis Sophia, or Books of the Saviour*, Book 1, Chap. 18.

the same collection, the soul of the Knower, ascending through these Spheres, delivers a resounding denial to the Rulers of Fate who would subject it to Destiny:

> Take your destiny! I come not to your regions from this moment onwards. I have become a stranger unto you for ever, being about to go unto the region of my inheritance.[13]

Another, similar account in which the Spheres are disturbed, thereby eliminating Fate can be found in the Nag Hammadi text "Trimorphic Protennoia":

> And the lots of Fate and those who apportion the domiciles were greatly disturbed over a great thunder. And the thrones of the Powers were disturbed, since they were overturned, and their King was afraid. And those who pursue Fate paid their allotment of visits to the path, and they said to the Powers, "What is this disturbance and this shaking that has come upon us through a Voice to the exalted Speech? And our entire habitation has been shaken, and the entire

---

[13] Ibid. Book 3, Chap. 112

circuit of the path of ascent has met with destruction, and the path upon which we go, which takes us up to the Archgenitor of our birth, has ceased to be established for us."[14]

That sacramental practice could unloose the bonds of Fate is attested to in the "Excerpts of Theodotus," a collection of Valentinian sayings recorded by Clement of Alexandria:

Until baptism, they say, Fate is effective, but after it the astrologers no longer speak the truth. It is not the bath alone that makes us free, but also the knowledge: who were we? what have we become? where were we? into what place have we been cast? whither are we hastening? from what are we delivered? what is birth? what is rebirth?[15]

Again and again we find this concept in the literature. The human is trapped within the World of

[14] Turner, John trans. "Trimorphic Protennoia." *The Nag Hammadi Library in English*, Robinson, James ed.

[15] Casey, Robert trans. Excerpta Ex Theodoto. http://www.hypotyposeis.org/papers/theodotus.htm

Forms, under the subject of the Archons, who rule
the Zodiac and the Planetary Spheres. This lack of
control over one's own set of circumstances leads to
what we refer to in Way-speak as the "Kenomic
Worldview." Modern prophet Philip K. Dick also
discusses an escape from astral determinism in the
Tractates Cryptica Scriptura:

> 49. Two realms there are, upper and lower. The
> upper, derived from hyperuniverse I or Yang, Form I
> of Parmenides, is sentient and volitional. The lower
> realm, or Yin, Form II of Parmenides, is mechanical,
> driven by blind, efficient cause, deterministic and
> without intelligence, since it emanates from a dead
> source. In ancient times it was termed 'astral
> determinism.' We are trapped, by and large, in the
> lower realm, but are through the sacraments, by
> means of the plasmate, extricated. Until astral
> determinism is broken, we are not even aware of it, so
> occluded are we. 'The Empire never ended.'

As Dick says, until we break this astral determinism,
we are so under its influence that we don't even
recognize it.

Through various ascent practices, represented in

This Way by the Greater Precepts or Renunciation of the Archons, we begin to recognize that we exist in this state, and may begin to address it. In essence, we begin to recognize that the Archons are themselves imperfect, and depending upon their influences as guides for Right Action will only ever have imperfect results. This is why we disregard what horoscope casters have to say, and use divinatory tools such as tarot cards as intended– as tools for self-discovery, not for determining future paths.

There is another, more practical reason for the admonition against fortune telling. The goal of the Way person in cultivating the Pleromic Worldview is to live as much as possible in the present moment. As part of life in the Kenoma, and modern life in general, we are commonly beset by "archonic" influences such as anxiety, depression, concern, which can weigh us down and cause us to indulge in another kind of "fortune telling." We become so worried about what "might" happen in any given situation, even something so far in the future or so complex in nature that we aren't able to discern the webs of cause and effect that may change before the event occurs.

How many times do we stay awake at night worrying or fretting about what might happen the next day, week, month or year? Isn't this "fortune telling"? Shouldn't we be sleeping instead? Indeed, a great variety of disorders and health problems arise when we fall under the spell of these Archonic powers that reside within and without of us, unable to live fully in the present moment because our head is full of the chattering of the Rulers of the World of Forms. These obsessive chatterings are the true Archonic Scriptures, chaotic and pointless, distracting and dangerous.

Doing contemplative practice is the best way to train the mind to rid itself of these "Archonic Scriptures" and regular practice will bring about peace and contentment.

10 +AWAKENING: A PRACTICE

This basic contemplative practice has proven effective in movement towards the awakening experience in its practitioners. It should by no means replace similarly effective practices which have already been established by the practitioner, or effective practices which are components of the practitioner's chosen spiritual community. It is offered as a possibility that has worked.

Establishing a Meditation Space. First, find a space where you can meditate. If you can help it, it should not be in your bedroom or kitchen or dining room or any area that has some other 'purpose.' If possible, devote an entire room or closet to meditative practice. If not possible, just make sure your space is clean and uncluttered and quiet, as the mind tends to reflect its external surroundings. It does not have to be completely sound-proof, just attempt to avoid loud noises or distractions. You may find it helpful to have some sacred imagery in your space— images of favorite spiritual leaders, candles, rosaries, a small altar or shrine, etc.– but even a bare room will do the trick.

When you have established your 'space,' make it distinct from the other areas within your living quarters by doing a ritual of some kind every time you enter or leave it. For example, use a small holy water lavabo and make the sign of the cross when entering or leaving. You might also ring a bell or kneel or say a small prayer. The idea is to distinguish this space from the rest of your house by creating an invisible border, which will help ground you and allow you to exist independently of the rest of your house during your meditative practice. If you cannot have a room or area set aside for this purpose, or if you are practicing outside, you can make do with visualizing a "border" between your sitting place and the surrounding environment, perhaps a circle or a square, and then acknowledging the division when you cross over the border.

Begin your meditative process whenever it works best for you. Some people have great success meditating early in the morning, but I find I get too sleepy. Start by crossing the border into your space, and then begin the session by 'addressing' the Limitless Light. Face the East and visualize a soft pink light filling the room or area, like the color of strawberry iced cream (this comes from Philip K. Dick). You are notifying the Pleroma that you are going to attempt communicating with it directly.

Preparing to Meditate. Now sit in a meditation posture. Full or half lotus are fine, but I prefer kneeling. Kneeling during meditation gives me the same energy as kneeling during prayer– you are becoming a receptive element, recognizing your role as an open and passive receptacle for the experience. Kneeling represents submission to the All. Of course, it can also be incredibly uncomfortable. Some people prefer this discomfort, as overcoming or ignoring it can be very illustrative, but I like to kneel on a cushion and place a wedge pillow between my calves and my butt. One can face the East, the direction of light and the rising sun, or the South, the direction of Wisdom, though the North and West are avoided in many spiritual traditions.

No matter your preferred position, POSTURE IS EXTREMELY IMPORTANT! In fact, one might say that one's posture is more important that one's position. You can actually injure your back with incorrect posture. Slumping forward can also make you drowsy. To assist you in correcting your posture, picture a taut string descending from heaven attached to the crown of your head (where the soft spot was when you were a baby). When the string is pulled up taught, the head should be tilted slightly forward and the spine should be straight. Press the tongue to the roof of your mouth. Your eyes can remain open or closed; closing your eyes makes it more likely that you will fall asleep. If you find a meditation position too painful, to the extent that you are concerned about injury (or are concerned about aggravating injuries incurred earlier in life), you may sit in a chair or lie on the floor.

Next, rest your hands lightly on your thighs. Take a few deep breaths, and you are ready to begin.

Meditation. Begin breathing slowly and steadily. Focus on your breath. There is no need to "count" your breaths, just allow them to flow naturally into one another. Breathe from the diaphragm, not the chest– your stomach should move in and out and your chest should remain still. Now, shift your awareness to a spot two inches below your navel. If it helps, make a spot at that point with a magic marker before you begin (this seems funny, but it works!). As you breathe in, mentally say the word "Christos" (pronounced KRĪSH-tos) As you breathe out, mentally say the word "Sophia" (pronounced so-FĪ-ya). In, Christos, stomach rises, out, Sophia, stomach falls. Christos, Sophia. Focus on your spot and repeat these words.

Invariably, thoughts will begin to arise and your mind will begin wandering. When you notice that your mind has begun wandering, say to yourself, "thinking," return your awareness to your spot and begin again with Christos, Sophia. No matter what sensation arises other than your Christos, Sophia and your spot, acknowledge it and move on. If you have an itch that distracts you, think, "itching" and move on, return your awareness to your spot and your breathing. If it does not go away, scratch it, but say "scratching the itch" and return to your spot and your breathing. If you find yourself slumping, say "slumping and straightening" and pull the imaginary line taught. Continue in this way, simply being, acknowledging all thoughts but letting them pass away.

You will find, after a while, that the instances of "thinking" etc. are fewer and fewer. You are opening an inner gate and cleaning your inner stables, so you might have some thoughts that are utterly mystifying. No matter how unusual or bizarre the thought, let it pass away as soon as you are aware you are thinking it. You might think, "I've always wanted to kill so-and-so," but do not be amazed; it is just a thought. Just say "thinking" and return to your spot and your breathing. Your mind might be muddled with problems stemming from work or your social life. Do not attribute the thoughts with any value, simply say "thinking" and let them fade away, returning your awareness to your spot and moving on.

Distractions During Meditation. Perhaps the most common distracting thought is the tendency to think, "this is really working, I'm doing it, my mind is empty!" It is very irritating to find one's self thinking these thoughts! But, one should not become irritated, one should simply say, "thinking" and return one's awareness to the spot, Christos, Sophia.

Sooner or later, after a week, a month or even a year, you might start experiencing "visions," hearing sounds, experiencing inner light shows. They might be utterly profound; you might see the Queen of Heaven in all of her radiant glory revealing the Keys of Wisdom. You might hear the answer to a question you have had for some time. Your experiences might be incredibly bizarre– I remember once I had an intense vision of a giant, spinning head of Mao Tse-Tung, and I still have no idea what to make of that!

It is good to have these experiences, because they mean you are progressing, but once again, they are not what you are after. You need to keep pushing beyond these visions, say "having a vision," or something similar, and return your focus to your spot and your breathing. Most likely you will find yourself amazed by the experience and you will think, "wow, a vision, this is amazing!" If this happens, acknowledge it is happening and return to your spot and to your breathing.

There is another common pitfall of regular practice. Soon after you feel as though you are progressing– it could be days, weeks or months– you will have a relapse. You will not be able to concentrate. Sitting quietly will become uncomfortable. It will be as though all of your progress was for nothing. This is not unusual or worrying– just keep at it! Eventually this will pass and you will be back to your normal level in no time.

If you practice in this way, your goal is Awakening. Your goal is not being told what awakening is by the Queen of Heaven– it is the DIRECT EXPERIENCE. Your goal is not to have wild visions, no matter how interesting or insightful they are. If you are simply interested in having visionary experiences, there are far easier ways to go about doing so. Everything that happens to you while meditating save awakening is a valueless distraction and should be seen as such. It is not something that you will think or imagine or be told, it is an actual experience you will have, you will absolutely know it when you have reached that point.

Ending a Meditation Session. One should stop meditating when one is satisfied, sleepy or too distracted. There is no real set amount of time to continue practicing, and there is absolutely no reason to force one's self to sit for a long time if one does not want to do so. Try starting with ten minutes a day, and gradually increase that time as you see fit. You will find at the beginning that those ten minutes seem like they take FOREVER, but stilling the mind also stills the mind's perception of time, so eventually one reaches a point where one finds that a meditation session has lasted for two hours even though one feels as though it is only been fifteen minutes.

When you are ready to stop, bring your awareness back to your eyes and sit quietly for a moment, coming back into your "waking" awareness. Then stand, facing the East, and stretch, getting any kinks out. Close with a short prayer. When you leave your meditation space, do not forget to "cross the threshold."

Finally, it is very helpful to keep a journal of your experiences, even if it is just, "sat for five minutes, got bored, stopped." Record any thoughts or sensations you found particularly interesting.

More advanced practitioners may find other practices valuable, such as Ascent practice or Kimetikos. These have been touched upon elsewhere, and will be elaborated in future volumes. However, these are practices best-suited for those interested in additional experience, and the practice given above should prove sufficient for the average student of This Way.

10 THE SELF: LEGGO MY EGO?

What to do with the self? The perennial question of spiritual seekers everywhere, hashed and rehashed dozens of times by those who claim the ego is bad mojo and needs elimination. Indeed, the idea that the ego should be excised has become an integral part of the religious dialogue. Let's have a look.

According to Buddhist phenomenology, the "self" as a unique entity does not exist. Instead, what humans percieve as "selfness" is actually the five skandhas, also known as "five heaps": form (rupa), sensation (vedana), perception (sanna), mental formations (sankhara) and consciousness (vinanna).

Coming to the realization that all of these skandhas are essentially ephemeral and changing is a key facet of Gautama's original teaching found in the Heart Sutra. Confusing one's "Self" with any one of the skandhas, or any combination thereof, is the root cause of desire and suffering in the world. At the

same time, consciously and mindfully focusing upon
and contemplating the impermanence of the
skandhas can bring the practitioner to the experience
of Nirvana through the elimination of self-ness:

> Avalokita, The Holy Lord and Bodhisattva, was
> moving in the deep course of the Wisdom which has
> gone beyond. He looked down from on high, He
> beheld but five heaps, and he saw that in their own-
> being they were empty.

> Here, Sariputra, form is emptiness and the very
> emptiness is form; emptiness does not differ from
> form, form does not differ from emptiness; whatever
> is form, that is emptiness, whatever is emptiness, that
> is form, the same is true of feelings, perceptions,
> impulses and consciousness....

> Therefore, Sariputra, it is because of his non-
> attainment that a Bodhisattva, through having relied
> on the Perfection of Wisdom, dwells without
> thought-coverings. In the absence of thought-
> coverings he has not been made to tremble, he has
> overcome what can upset, and in the end he attains to

Nirvana.

Remarkably, the *Secret Book of John* also lists five "powers," or Archons, that govern the interaction of the human with the Kosmos:

The one who governs perceptions: Archendekta

The one who governs reception: Deitharbathas

The one who governs imagination: Oummaa

The one who governs integration: Aachiaram

The one who governs impulse: Riaramnacho.

The skandhas and the governors of perception have an almost one-to-one correspondence, though we present them in a different order. This is not to suggest that the author of the *Secret Book of John* was familiar with the skandhas or that this was originally intended; however, it is certainly an interesting thematic correspondence:

Form: Rupa:: Impulse: Riaramnacho

Sensation: Vedana:: Reception: Deitharbathas

Perception: Sanna:: Perception: Archendekta

Mental Formations: Sankhara:: Imagination: Oumma

Consciousness: Vinanna:: Integration: Aachiaram

Since the qualities of these Archons are so patently concerned with phenomenology, and as the Buddhist skandhas are an aggregation of various experiences as perceived by humans through the senses but are not essentially real, so the Archons also represent unreal experiences within the World of Forms which lead the human into pleasure, desire, grief and fear:

The four chief demons are: Ephememphi, associated with pleasure, Yoko, associated with desire, Nenentophni, associated with distress, Blaomen, associated with fear. Their mother is Esthesis-Zouch-Epi-Ptoe.

Out from these four demons come passions: From distress arises Envy, jealousy, grief, vexation, Discord, cruelty, worry, mourning.

From pleasure comes much evil And unmerited pride,

And so forth.

From desire comes Anger, fury, bitterness, outrage, dissatisfaction And so forth.

From fear emerges Horror, flattery, suffering, and shame.

There is no indication within Sethian thought that the Self does not exist. Indeed, the Archons involved in the creation and perception of the ephemeral world serve to occlude the Self at their center. This does not mean that invisible aliens are crawling all over your soul; these are not "Body thetans." They are, instead, the impermanent things that impede one's ability to experience the psychospiritual state we call "dwelling in gnosis." They are the roadblock on the path to self-knowledge, and in This Way, through mindful contemplation on them, one does not discover that there is no self, but instead discovers that essential spark of the Universal Self that exists under the surface of the World of Forms.

11 ABIDING CONSTANCY

If one word could be used to describe the vast majority of human activity over the last few centuries, it would surely be *"reactionary."* Everyone needs to have his or her say, everyone needs something to happen, everyone needs his or her opinion heard and accepted, and it needs to happen immediately. Nine tenths of the problems people have would disappear if we could all embrace the quality of patience– patience with one another, patience with ourselves, patience with the actions of the Logos and Sophia in the World of Forms.

What is the nature of contemplative practice and meditation? It is the act of **constant abiding**, patiently training the spirit to accept the inbreaking of the Pleroma into this World. When we live in patience with ourselves and our communities and those with whom we act on a day-to-day basis, we begin to transform our entire lives into acts of contemplation.

How does abiding constacy manifest in our person?

1. We put aside our expectations and eliminate hope. This sounds different than it manifests, because when we talk about "eliminating hope," we don't mean replacing it with hopelessness. Instead, we mean accepting each moment for what it is.

2. We renounce fortune-telling. Rather than project expectations onto some oblique future state, we allow ourselves to reflect on no more than a moment into the past and a moment into the future.

3. We trust in the Logos and Sophia, and trust that our practice will have results, even if they are not immediately noticeable.

How does abiding constancy manifest in our interactions with others?

1. Should we choose to share the Way with another, we wait for that person to come to his or her own conclusions, patiently, without making assumptions about his or her own

      spiritual understanding.

2. We accept that we will never completely agree with any Path, and avoid comparing our best qualities with another Path's worst qualities.

3. We pause and wait a while before making decisions, especially in reaction to something major, even when it seems that immediate action is required.

This is in no way meant to encourage the overly sentimentalized and wrong-headed concept that "everything happens for a reason;" often, it means mindfully accepting the fact that circumstances are quite often without any kind of reason within this World of Forms. It means mindfully accepting that not everything needs to be a reaction to something else. It also requires a sense of vigilance and awareness on the part of the practitioner, and the ability to discriminate between situations in which abiding constancy applies and those in which waiting would not be the correct approach.

As a practice in Abiding Constancy, the Way person may wish to try the following exercise: when one becomes anxious or feels impatient, focus on what was happening no more than five minutes prior to that moment, and what may happen no more than five minutes from it. "Five minutes ago, I was walking to work. Five minutes from now, I will be answering my e-mail." Try to maintain this focus, so that eventually one begins to develop a ten minute consciousness. If this is too difficult, try a half-hour. After a while, try reducing the amount of time. Can you limit your consciousness to a single minute?

12 SILENT AGENCY

As a Silent Agent, the Way person can practice alone or within a spiritual community. This Way can be incorporated into one's personal approach to religious practice within any community provided the community meets certain requirements. This is not a question of value, or of placing value judgments on other systems– it is simply a matter of compatibility.

A Way person may find a spiritual home in any church, sangha or other organization with the following prerequisites:

1. The community must express the value of the Four Virtues of Inquiry, Compassion, Humility and Service in some form in its teachings.
2. The organization must have room in its paradigm for some form of contemplative practice.

3. The organization must provide a context into which both the Logos and Sophia may proceed.

4. The organization requires no vow or credal commitment with which the Way Gnostic is not comfortable.

Provided these conditions are present, a Way person should feel perfectly comfortable adjusting his or her own outward expressions of spiritual understanding as needed. Indeed, a great deal– if not the majority– of mainstream and orthodox religious organizations fit this bill. Even those organizations who are vocally opposed to outmoded understandings of "Gnosticism" can provide a spiritual community to the Way person, who understands that an organization is still a collection of individuals, and one is attached to the rules and regulations of a community only to the extent that one allows for one's self.

A Way person may even choose a vocation within any spiritual organization in which he or she feels so called, provided one's vocation is not at odds with the above basic components of this path.

If one finds a spiritual home into which one's path as a Way person can be integrated, it should by no means be kept a secret from other members of the community. Nonetheless, in keeping with the third virtue of the Way, one should keep a **Silent Agency** as a Way person, expressing as little as necessary, and only if directly asked. This is important not as a matter of 'keeping secrets,' but is intended as a way to express proper respect and regard for faith traditions in which we might find refuge. For this reason, debate with others about the specifics of spiritual theory and practice is always highly discouraged. One should feel free to disagree with one's spiritual community, but unless one's values or virtues are compromised, there should be no need for this kind of exchange. In this Way, we hold the understanding that the best method of instruction is example, so let our actions speak to other members of our community.

We stress at this time that one's participation in this Way does not grant one any kind of superiority over other individuals or their own spiritual understanding. Remember, **not everyone needs gnosis**, and it is not our place to judge the spiritual experiences of other people. Instead, let us share the inherent beauty of the quest for gnosis through our *deeds and actions*, regardless of where we happen to be stationed.

13 MAKE YOUR LIFE YOUR PRACTICE

A final admonition to the Way person: how many times have we heard it from the self-satisfied who know better than we because they've established some repetitive habits: "you can't be religious/spiritual unless you practice. You have to Do The Work." They then proceed, rather smugly in many cases, to explain how those who "do the work" are far superior to those who "merely" study or maintain a spiritual worldview.

This is a fallacious conceit, and a false dichotomy. It is based on a notion that one should set aside certain times for spiritual practice, be those times Sunday mornings, or an hour here and there for meditation, and that those who have done so are spiritually superior to those who have not. If "doing the work" means going to church on Sunday or meditating once a day, then "doing the work" becomes completely useless, because **the whole point of the spiritual teachings of Jesus and the Buddha is to make your entire life your practice.**

Indeed, we may justifiably reason that what many people consider "the work" is merely peripheral to a healthy spiritual life. The Eucharist, for example, and the various other sacraments, are **the least important** aspects of the Christian tradition. Meditation and the search for enlightenment are **the least important** aspects of Buddhism. Focusing on "the work," and insisting that setting time aside for practice is an imperative, actually becomes detrimental towards the assistance we may be able to provide other sentient beings, because it quickly devolves into an insistence that salvation is impossible without so doing– "Only those who have been baptized/have taken communion/have achieved satori can be saved." In this era, if we insist that salvation is only possible through ritual practice or some kind of work, we will alienate far more than we will assist.

In many ways, this is in direct opposition to statements made to the contrary in our historical scriptures, or indeed, *in this very text*. However, it is the purpose of this Way to evolve these traditions by interpreting them according to modern sensibilities– we do not claim that what was correct in the Fourth

Century can still apply in the modern day.

Regardless of what has been said by those involved in these traditions, salvation cannot come through mere practice, and cannot be reduced to "Salvation = Eucharist + Prayer + ..." If one views spiritual understanding as a spectrum, these practices are very minor points on that spectrum, insignificant next to the amount of time we are given to express our gnosis throughout the course of our existences within the World of Forms.

What, then, is the most important? It is overcoming the Kenomic Worldview and establishing the reign of the Pleroma within.

This is not to say, of course, that ritual and prayer and contemplative practice don't have their place– that they are effective and valid cannot be argued by any reasonable student of spirituality. They are, however, pointless if they are the focus of one's spiritual pursuits, if one's entire life does not become one's spiritual practice. If one makes one's life one's practice, the formulaic methodologies of ritualism, prayer and meditation can be seamlessly incorporated into an holistic experience without recourse to empty specificity. Gnosis, according to this Way, is primarily Information plus Wisdom, integrated with

Insight. Through the Grace of the Limitless Light, Gnosis can emerge within one without any methodology other than study and application of that study to every aspect of one's life, from brushing the teeth in the morning to drifting off to sleep at night, a far more fulfilling and delightful "practice" than forcing one's self through a series of tedious exercises only available to a few who are fortunate enough to have access to extra time or geographical resources.

If one never attends church, never meditates, but instead spends one's entire existence studying and incorporating *gnosis* into one's every thought and action, one has accomplished so much more than the average spiritual imperialist, who cherry-picks "practices" from various traditions, or the average religious show-offs who wear their collars out drinking and never shut up about how they've encouraged so many people to "do the work."

Don't "do the work"– **spiritual practice, nine times out of ten, is a complete waste of time**, time that could be spent sleeping in or sharing a meal with loved ones or playing with your dogs. If you are inclined towards idleness regarding ritual practice but have a firm conviction regarding the study of the cultivation of gnosis, and its application within every breath you take, every interaction you have with

others, and every word you utter, you can safely
ignore the platitudes of those who insist that their
actions are more valid than your reason for being.

ABOUT THE AUTHOR

"Vell, Zaphod's **just zis guy , you know**?"

> Gag Halfrunt, *The Hitchhiker's Guide to the Galaxy* by
> Douglas Adams